# Lose Life

### *Devotional t*
#### *(Part 1*

## Peter Walker

*'Sleep baby sleep*
*Now that the night is over*
*And the sun comes like a god…'*

'New Sensation', INXS

## www.1peter1three.weebly.com

*I dedicate this devotional to Adam Dawson, a pastor to the youth of Grace Church, a great husband, father, friend and man of God.*

# Introduction

The teen years are tough! You are more adult than often people give you credit for, and yet also in the throes of change and progress that needs deep and wide understanding – on your part, and that of others.

Let's keep it real from the get-go: You got to understand that adults have been teens, and very few of them treat you – or limit you – just to be a pain in the neck. We as adults don't always get it right, but honestly, most of us are trying to keep you steady and on course so that you can be all you can be, experience all that God has for you, be powerful and effective in this broken world, and fight injustice and immorality – rather than be another casualty of injustice and immorality! So be patient with us also!:)

I became a committed follower of Jesus at 16 years old. Although I had grown up with Christian parents, I had also grown up on the mission field, where our church was small and organic, not in a network, no youth group, and little support. So when I decided to follow Jesus – rather than just allow Him to follow me – I had no Christian friends. I had a lot of so-called friends, but none that were committed to Jesus. So when I stood on my faith-feet, I was in a battle instantly. And it was bloody. The winds were blowing. Friends were dropping like flies, scornful looks from the pretty girls, weirded-out amigos by my new Jesus thing, etc. Some parents even banned me from hanging out with their kids (my friends) because of my 'religion'. So on top of my teenage status and stage in life, I was thrown into quite another challenge: that of being different, misunderstood and rejected for my faith. God has been so good and gracious to me, and some of my most intimate times with God were in that dark and lonely space and time. Truly. I thank God from the bottom of my heart that he threw a spear through the heart of my teenage buzz, and called me to the cross.

This devotional consists of 20 entries (daily or weekly or whenever!), and a few links to some videos where I speak to verses or themes. There is space to jot down your own thoughts, and I hope you do. Scribble all over the place with what the Lord is speaking to you.

After you finish this devotional, check out the follow-up, called, *'Walk The Talk!'*

Bless you!

Peter Walker

**# 1**   *(day and date:_____)*

*'So we fix our eyes not on what is seen, but on what is unseen. For what is seen is temporary, but what is unseen is eternal'*
II Corinthians 4:18

When I was 16 and in the throes of jungle life that is adolescence and school, Jesus pressed in on me. I remember he quietly but strongly said to my heart, *'Peter, you know I am true, but you are living like I am not true.'* I started to cry because I knew my number was up! I thank God for calling me out, getting me real and honest with myself about my belief in Him, setting my feet on a tough but glorious path that is the narrow one. Above verse meant a lot to me in my lonely walk for the first while, as I lost more friends than I made, because of my renewed commitment to Jesus. I had to lift my eyes from 'others' in school, and fix my eyes on the eternal.

Do you find school a scary place to stand up for what is true, and for your faith in Jesus? Yes, it is! But if you can wisely, quietly, strongly begin to stand with Christ in your school setting, He will honor you.

*'He who acknowledges me before men, the Son of Man will acknowledge him before the angels of God.'*
Luke 12:8

Devotional Activity:
Today take a quiet moment, 2 minutes somewhere alone, close your eyes and lift your hands and say, 'Jesus, you are truly my best friend!' (John 15:15)

**# 2**     *(day and date:_____)*

**'Though my father and mother forsake me, the Lord will receive me'** Psalm 27:10

Maybe this is your experience, of having been let down or abandoned by your father, or mother. If so, you hold a very significant place in the heart of God. In fact, God goes so far as to make clear to us that 'religion he considers pure', is to care for the fatherless (James 1:27). He also speaks to this in Hosea 14:3, and many other places. Though you, maybe, and/or some of your friends, have experienced this brokenness in life, this is due to the broken life we live in. You are not less, but, in fact, set apart by God for special blessing. Jesus is the great redeemer of our sorrow, to make gold out of it. He can even make life out of death – his ultimate expression of repair and restoration.

Devotional Activity:
Find something on your school supplies – a pencil case, back of a notebook, bag strap, whatever – and write with permanent pen today's verse: Psalm 27:10 (above). Maybe cast your eye over the verse a couple times today, and pray for a friend or two.

# 3    (*day and date:_____*)

*'Blessed are you when people insult you, persecute you and falsely say all kinds of evil against you because of me... great is your reward in heaven...'* Matthew 5:11-12

We work really hard as Christians to get along well with those who are not Christians. This is good and wise (II Corinthians 8:21; Matthew 5:16). However, we need to be careful that our efforts to be 'good' do not become simply 'compromise' or fear to be true to our faith, or a desire to simply fit in. This is not the same thing as 'letting our good deeds shine before men.' God calls us to make efforts in goodness, so that He gets the glory, not so we get an easy ride. For this reason it is important to not only live the grace of Jesus, but to let people know you believe in Jesus, that you are a Christian. This may make things a little tough at times, and that is when today's verse really makes sense to us.

Devotional Activity:
Think and pray about this question today: When people are trying to get you to look at something (maybe on their phone) that you should not be looking at, do you say, 'No, that's not cool', or do you say, 'No, I don't look at that kind of thing because I'm a Christian.'

**'Flee the evil desires of youth and pursue righteousness, faith, love and peace, along with those who call on the Lord out of a pure heart.'** II Timothy 2:22

I memorize a lot of scripture. I often think of the fact that the 'word of God' is the only offensive weapon in the 'armor of God' (Ephesians 6:17). If you are not quoting, referencing or basing on scripture, what is the real quality of what's coming out of your mouth? So, I love verses that have easy references, like above. Say the reference a couple times (lots of 2's in there), with a desire to really memorize.

But, more significantly about above verse, are the following: firstly, the admonishment to 'flee' evil desires. Don't reason yourself out of them. Don't walk parallel to them. Turn your back and walk the opposite direction. Secondly – and I love this second part of the verse - to go after righteousness not just with church-goers or people who even call on the Lord; but those who call on the Lord with *'out of a pure heart'*.

Devotional Activity:
Take a pen and paper and write down the names of Christian friends that you think are cool. Now make another list of names of those Christian friends that you feel *'call on the Lord out of a pure heart'*. This is not judgmental, but wisdom. Now love on both sets of Christian friends, but take example from the latter.

**# 5**   *(day and date:_____)*

**'Be either hot or cold. If you are lukewarm I will spit you out of my mouth.'** Revelation 3:16

Often people tell me they have no problem with what Jesus said, but they just don't believe He was God… I tell these people that this is because they do not know what Jesus said. If they read the bible they would realize that he was full of powerfully challenging and offensive comments (to our flesh). We should all have problems with what Jesus said.

As a young dude you have a great opportunity to calibrate your walk with God, now and forevermore. We need to 'fly our flag' honestly, and clearly. It is so much easier to be a Christian head-on, than to be a fluffy nice guy church-goer who seems kinda like, well, not sure maybe goes to church? Not only will your testimony be vulnerable, your very walk with Christ is vulnerable (see above verse).

Devotional Activity:
Take a few minutes today to ask Jesus to give you courage to walk with him honestly before others. Even Paul asked for prayer for courage (Ephesians 6:19-20; Philippians 1:20), as did Peter and others (Acts 4:29). If you are scared to be strong, you are in good company! Pray to Lord for courage.

**# 6**   *(day and date:_____)*

*'All souls are mine.'* Ezekiel 18:4

There are 2 perspectives or realities about our life as Christians here in the world. On the one hand, we are 'aliens' here. We are told in scripture that there is a kingdom here that is not the Lord's kingdom, run by a 'prince of darkness', and that our citizenship is in heaven. And so on the one hand when we feel lost and lonely as Christians here, it is because we are lost and lonely as Christians here!:) But… that is more of a spiritual positioning due to the war of darkness and light. On the other hand, as Christians we most truly belong here, and have rights here, and are 'at home'. Why? Because 'the earth is the Lord's (our Father's), and everything in it… and ALL who live in it.' (Psalm 24:1). And, in today's verse, God says, 'all souls are mine!' (not the devil's). So our Father is everyone's true Father, and darkness trespasses here, not light!

Devotional Activity:
Take a minute to look up some of these verses that are referenced above: Ezekiel 18:4; Psalm 24:1; John 14:30 (but John 16:11); John 17:15; Ephesians 6:10-13; Philippians 3:20

**# 7**  *(day and date:_____)*

*'God has chosen to make known… the glorious riches of this mystery, which is Christ in you, the hope of glory.'* Colossians 1:27

Throughout the ages and journey of the Old Testament – wandering in the desert for 40 years, starving, parched, wars, loss, rituals, sacrifices, sorrows – all of this came to its full meaning - not only in Christ's life, but in this: Christ in you!

So is Christ in you? Does the 'hope of glory' blow through your soul like a fresh mist? Have you taken hold of that for which many hundreds and thousands of people have yearned and died, but never could fully know? Have you raised your hands to heaven and rejected all sin and darkness in your life, and asked God to pour out Jesus Christ into your very soul? In that moment and reality there is the full consummation of the 'glorious riches' of God's most treasured truth.

Devotional Activity:
Take a few quiet minutes today and ask the Lord to give you a fresh vision of what it means to have 'Christ in you'. (Matthew 22:36-40; Deuteronomy 6:4-5; Leviticus 19:18)

**# 8**    *(day and date:_____)*

*'If you declare with your mouth, "Jesus is Lord" and believe in your heart that God raised him from the dead, you will be saved. For it is with your heart that you believe and are justified, and it is with your mouth that you profess your faith and are saved.'* Romans 10:9-10

Do you profess your faith? There is something deep and required by Jesus about not only believing, but professing our faith. It is because others have professed their faith, that you came to hear and believe. Jesus said, *'You are the light of the world…people do not light a lamp and put it under a bowl. Instead they put it on its stand, and it gives light to everyone…'*
(Matthew 5:14-15)

Jesus will not let us away with simply saying and singing that He is the light of the world (referencing John 1:9 and 8:12). Jesus says, 'No, Pete, actually *you* are the light of the world! Now get out there and shine it!' (Matthew 5:14)

Devotional Activity:
Ask Jesus in prayer today to show you how he has equipped you personally to profess His name. It is not the same way for everyone. Ask Jesus to begin to show you your way.

**# 9**   *(day and date:_____)*

*'The name of the Lord is a strong tower; the righteous run into it and are safe.'* Proverbs 18:10

Two insights hit me with this verse. Firstly, the name of the Lord is a safe place. You have a fortified tower – the most safe, a completely unassailable place – in the name of the Lord Jesus. His name, your trap door to your soul's destiny, heaven and all things new. When down to your last, just close your eyes and whisper His name: Jesus.

Secondly, the righteous run into it (His name) and are safe. Not *because* they are righteous, but rather they become righteous because they run into his name. Church is full, not of good people, but of saved people. And in many respects, Christians (you and me!) are those people that really are not good (I Corinthians 1:27; Luke 5:31). Jesus said, 'there is no one good…' (Luke 18:19) – but this is because he was speaking to the self-righteous. Others are referred to as good peeps, even pagans (Acts 2:1-2). So in some respects, my brother and sister, on the spectrum of just good deeds, thoughts and dispositions, many atheists, pagans and others rank naturally higher than you and me, they are 'better people'. But to be 'righteous' before God, we all need to run into His name.

<u>Devotional Activity</u>:
Who of your non-Christian friends are pretty good peeps? Write their names down, and pray to ask God to reveal Himself to them for 'righteousness', like he did for Cornelieus (Acts 2).

# 10  *(day and date:_____)*

*'… you will be like God, knowing good and evil.'*
Genesis 3:5-6

In every lie (powerful lie) there are shreds of truth.
The devil is a liar (John 8:44), and in the utterance of
his first lie to man there was some truth in it. He said
in rebelling against God's command we would come
to know good from evil. There is much truth in this.
We do know – and struggle deeply with knowing –
good from evil. This knowledge, however, brings us
deep distress in our lives.  In fact, Ecclesiastes says
with the increase of knowledge is the increase of
sorrow (Ecclesiastes 1:18). So the devil was right
about the 'knowing', he just didn't tell us this
knowledge would be the source of our agony, and
part of a broken soul. This is why Jesus said that the
kingdom of heaven belongs not to the
knowledgeable, but to the innocent (Luke 18:16).

There is much pressure in your life at this stage to
know more, experience more, touch, taste and see
more. Remember, that 'knowledge' is not power.
Innocence before God – in fact 'not knowing' earthly
darkness, is power. The most powerful of all men,
and the most influential with all people – even
prostitutes and gangsters – was a man who 'knew no
sin.' (II Corinthians 5:21). You don't have to 'know' or
have experienced what other people have, to be a
leader amongst those same people. It's not what you
know, it's who you know.

<u>Devotional Activity</u>:
Ask yourself, 'Do I really believe that Jesus is the light, source and power of everything true?' A couple verses to consider (John 1:9; 8:12; 11:25-26; 10:9; 14:6,15)

# 11 (*day and date:*_____)

*'My eyes are ever on the Lord, for He alone can free my feet from the snare.'* Psalm 25:15

Jesus wants us to lean in, move towards, seek, knock, yearn (Psalm 84:2; Matthew 7:7; Philippians 3:10-15; Hebrews 4:11). Now this is actually good news. Why? Well, in your faith have you ever found yourself not really 'feeling it'? Have you ever got a little doubtful or even downcast because your feelings were not exactly jiving with your faith, or your emotions were not jumping like worship on Sunday morning? Jesus does not call us to 'fake it till we make it', but rather to just humbly, quietly, walk towards His light. When we see it and feel His warmth, we 'gaze'; when there is cloud cover, we just steadily move on, and 'seek'.

*'One thing I ask of the Lord… that I may dwell in the house of the Lord <u>to gaze</u> upon the beauty of the Lord, and <u>to seek</u> Him…'*
Psalm 27:4

<u>Devotional Activity</u>:
Take 4 or 5 minutes to look up every verse that is listed above. The first and last one are written for you, but look up the verses that are noted above but now written out.

**# 12**  *(day and date:_____)*

*'Take heart... your sins are forgiven.'* Matthew 9:2

This is a powerful statement of Jesus', and a gift to
this lame man – but it is not what this lame man
came to Jesus for! He came for his legs to be healed,
not for his soul to be healed. Aha! - this is where we
often are so short-sighted. Jesus, in His mercy and
grace, will often reach to that thing that our soul
needs – and address that with us – before He
answers our 'want' prayers, or even other needs.
This man did need healing of his body, but Jesus
knew that in order to have the fullness of life (John
10:10), and to fully enjoy bodily health the way God
intended, this man needed his heart healed, his
eternity set. We need our sins forgiven.

Devotional Activity:
You might be praying for things right now, and really
looking to see where and how God is answering that
prayer. God hears you! (Matthew 6:8). But what,
maybe, is Jesus speaking back to you? Maybe He
wants to give you something other first, before giving
you what you are asking for. Sometimes this is even
a gift of repentance. Is Jesus calling you to repent for
something? If not, what is He saying to you?

**# 13**  *(day and date:_____)*

*'Where is the wise person? Where is the teacher of the law? Where is the philosopher of this age? Has not God made foolish the wisdom of the world?'* I Corinthians 1:20

I loved apologetics when I first felt the Lord call me at the age of 16. Apologetics is, I suppose, the 'rational' or mind-based stuff in Christianity. The discoveries and amazing things that 'prove' the truth of scripture. My cousin, Charlie, is a great apologetic, and if you enjoy this important aspect of Christianity, check out his stuff, maybe shoot him a line!
**http://www.alwaysbeready.com**

However, there is another side of our faith, my compadres, that is 'foolishness in the eyes of the world' (I Corinthians 1:18). Jesus allowed people to consider Him not only foolish, but demon-possessed (Matthew 12:24). We considered Jesus 'stricken by God' (Isaiah 53:4). Our real power comes not through persuasive words (I Corinthians 2:2), but through, in humility, standing with Jesus and saying we know Him (Luke 12:4-5, 8-9). So yes, fill your mind with good things, intelligent things, Greek, Hebrew and many, many answers, no problemo. But remember, the purpose of all true knowledge leads us to subject even 'answers' to the spirit of God, and to actually walk with Him - not to just have answers 'about' Him (Ephesians 3:16-19; Colossians 1:27; II Corinthians 10:3-5; Philippians 4:6-7).

Devotional Activity:
Loads of verses up there, look 'em all up!:)

**# 14** *(day and date:_____)*

*'... from infancy you have known the Holy Scriptures, which are able to make you wise for salvation through faith in Christ Jesus.'* II Timothy 3:15

The more open Jesus became about His identity, so to speak, the more endangered His life became. Jesus eluded questions (Luke 20:3-8), silenced dark or untimely testimonies (Luke 4:35), and ducked and dived a bit (John 5:13). I love this about His life and ministry, it was gritty and a lot like real life, just using one's head to outwit the enemy and hold things at bay. As things progressed, however, and Jesus had run the course of His calling, He began to let things about Himself settle with people. Pilate asked Him if He was the King of the Jews, and Jesus said, *'It is as you say.'* (Luke 23:3) His number was up now, identifying Himself fully in the face of Caesar, religious nuts, and the spiritual realms. They crucified Him.

There is a time to slip, slide, duck and dive. There really is. God Himself will block passages at times (Acts 16:6). However, there is also a time to be a little bolder about standing with Jesus. This is not a religious thing, or an equation (like trying to be radical by *(fill in the blank)*). No, don't try to be 'Rad', just get to know Jesus with discipline, daily bible reading, fellowshipping with the church, and quietly, consistently changing your life to look like His. How? By obedience! (John 14:15) Change what you say, what you do, your prayer life, and invite a friend to church!

<u>Devotional Activity</u>:
Don't be 'Rad', be real! Just know Christ and walk with Him every day. Look this verse up and write it on something, and go over it 10 times a day, chapter and verse, till it is branded like a favorite song on your mind: Psalm 73:25-26

**'The kingdom of heaven is like a treasure buried in a field. The man goes and sells everything he owns to buy that field.'** Matthew 13:44

This is the shortest parable in the bible – one verse! You gotta love that! And what a powerful, loaded parable it is! Listen, not only does this describe the intensity of the exchange for the 'kingdom of heaven' (EVERYTHING he owned), and therefore calibrate for us the worth of the kingdom of heaven, but it also tells us something deep and true about that treasure here on earth. It is not a treasure seen or valued by others (primarily). It is buried! It is not in sight! So when your peeps look confused at you for this faith you have, you hold, you prize, and they don't see it, that's perfectly in keeping with the nature of this prize. It is buried. Out of view.

Jesus constantly defied us in our desire to be wise in the eyes of the world (John 8:3; I Corinthians 1:18; 2:2). I used to think if I could just perform a miracle, I would not, could not, be considered a freak of (faith) nature. But Jesus cast out demons, and instead of people recognizing His truth, they said He did this because He himself had a demon! (Matthew 12:24) Jesus raised the dead… and they decided because of this power, they needed to 'plot His death' (John 11:45-53). Seeing is not always believing. In fact, seeing the power of God, sometimes exposes to someone that they really are not open to believing whether they see or not, and it triggers much hostility.

Devotional Activity:
Today's activity is a simple one (always the hardest!:)) Simply recognize that to stand with Jesus is 'foolishness in the eyes of the world' (and see I Corinthians 1:27). He is what we see with the eyes of our heart. He made it that way. We see light in His light (Psalm 36:9). You can't prove it! But thank God you can see it. Walk humbly in this revelation, and pray God opens the eyes of others.

**# 16**  (*day and date:*_____)

**'The bridegroom was a long time in coming, and they all became drowsy and fell asleep.'** Matthew 25:5

Today's verse is from the parable of the 10 virgins, which describes 5 of them being ready when the bridegroom came, and 5 of them not being ready. (This dude was about to marry 5 girls, therefore! This can only be the delusion of a man who has not yet attempted marriage with 1!) Anyway, moving swiftly along… Jesus spoke often about 'waiting' on Him, and waiting on God, and patience, and waiting some more. Did I mention 'waiting'? (Isaiah 40:31) Why? Not to exasperate us, as it might actually feel. But rather to work into our spirit, our soul, our eternal destiny, the deepest value of God – to know Him, to be in Him, to be one with Him (John 17:3; 21). We have got to understand, God does not need us to get things done. He *wants* us to have the fullness of life that He intended, and that is not knowing *about* him, or having a good life; it is, rather, simply knowing and being with Him.

And here's the deal. The deepest, sweetest experiences of God that you will have, the most intimate, those kinds that speak to His eternal darkness (Psalm 139:11), the mystery of morning darkness (Amos 4:13), are those where you are with Him, and not with an agenda. Not answered prayer, so to speak; but Jesus and your togetherness with him the actual prayer and the answer (Psalm 73:25-26).

<u>Devotional Activity</u>:
Just sit and be with God for a few minutes. Close your eyes and relax. Just think on Jesus, and sit with Him (Psalm 46:10).

**'... It is to one's glory to overlook an offense.'**
Proverbs 19:11

Teens are pretty extreme dudes and dudettes. We love that about you! But one challenging thing (of many) in this 'extreme' era of your life, are 'extreme' reactions. Teens can be the most reasonable and even virtuous and forgiving people, but they can also be quick to judge, begrudge, note and bank an 'offense'. You agree? Maybe you've been offended and that's for real. And God cares. But you're not going to answer for that. Here's what you will answer for: if you can, by God's grace, overlook an offense (forgive) and you choose not to.

Now, if an offense is truly a matter of folly in someone and against you, maybe you need some guidance about forgiving, yes, but changing your friend circle a little bit. Remember, we are called to plug into those people who call on the Lord 'out of a pure heart' (II Timothy 2:22). Get guidance, and get wiser friends! But there are other offenses that maybe, for whatever reason – hurt, insecurity, jealousy – you are choosing to not forgive; or maybe you are making an 'offense' out of nothing. This, my compadre, needs repentance on your part.

Devotional Activity: Is there someone you need to forgive and forget? (i.e. with wisdom change your hangin' patterns with this person). You know who it is! Talk to someone today about a plan of action. Is there someone who has offended you – but not really? (i.e. it is your jealousy or insecurity that is causing you to be a little cold towards them?) Then take your own selfish little soul by the scruff of the neck, and say to self, 'No! I will rise, forgive, forget and grow in Christ!' (II Corinthians 10:3-5)

**# 18**  *(day and date:_____)*

*'... All authority in heaven and on earth has been given to me...'* Matthew 28:18

GK Chesterton (1874-1936) said, 'The best book I ever wrote, is the one I haven't written.' This, bizarrely, speaks to one reason why I don't get tattoos. Let me explain. I told my brother a couple years ago that if I got a tattoo, it would be the above verse. Since then, however, the next verse I come across always strikes me as the most important one, of tattoo-significance… and so on and so on. I now have about 40 verses in my head (and counting), that if I went the tattoo route, would all have to be included. And I'm thinking probably the best verse – or tattoo – is the one I haven't yet come across… So I've decided to leave all the verses in the Bible, and make efforts this side of glory to 'print' them on my heart and mind, in spirit and truth (John 6:63; Psalm 119:11). I don't have enough skin for the tattoo game.

It is an incredible thing to settle in your mind today that 'all authority' – not just in heaven, but here on earth – belongs to Jesus Christ. The 'prince of this world', Jesus tells us, 'stands defeated.' (John 16:11) Truly, *'It is finished.'* (John 19:30). So like the end of any war, there is damage on all sides, collateral, residual breakage and pain and suffering, but it is over. Peace is going to grow slowly, repair, restore, descend fully on all sides. This is our walk in this dark world now. The game is over. Sin and death are done. But we walk through rubble till that glorious day.

<u>Devotional Activity</u>:
Pray for one friend today who does not know Jesus.
Ask Jesus to open the eyes of their heart to see Him.

**'...Are you able to drink the cup that I am about to drink?...'** Matthew 20:22

We live in a celebrity age. You can make an idol of your self with social media and then sit and stare at yourself all day long. James and John got a rush to the head (well, actually their mom did), trying to bag a scholarship to the most prestigious school in the universe: the throne room of God. Jesus was so gentle, as always, but terrifying in his response. They wanted greatness from Him, with Him, but were unaware that greatness in His kingdom was through the door of crucifixion.

If Jesus could grant you all the fame and fortune you ever wanted, even in and through church culture and circles, but He tagged on the end of this deal that one day you would be crucified, I think you, like me, might decline this road of glory, and prefer to be that happy 'doorkeeper' in the courts of God (Psalm 84:10).

So what is it we are looking for in fame and fortune? Well, there is a dark side of us that is looking for 'worship' because we want to be God (Genesis 3:5-6; Matthew 4:9). But we also have simply a fearful side, where we are seeking safety. Fame and fortune in this world look and feel like a safe place – comfort, smiles, favor, friends. So, repent of the former (worship), and regarding the latter (safety), see below activity!

<u>Devotional Activity</u>:
Jesus is our only safe place. Seriously! Not fame, not fortune, not even 'safety' is safe, if you know what I mean (Luke 12:13-21). His name *is* the strong tower. In His name we are safe! (Proverbs 18:10) Make Christ your dwelling place. This is a faith thing. This is spirit. (John 6:63; 17:3)

**'...Are you the one who is to come, or should we expect someone else?...'** Mark 11:3

John the Baptist in prison, and soon to be beheaded, sends word to Jesus asking if He really is the Savior. Now, John's whole life had been built around testifying to Jesus, saying that He was the Savior. Now, end of the road, he seems to doubt everything. Kinda like Peter doubted when only a step away from Jesus, walking – still standing – on water (Matthew 14:22-33).

Your faith will ebb and flow. It is a living thing. It is not something you bag once for all. It battles daily against internal pressures, external circumstances, spiritual assaults from the devil, spiritual tests from God. We don't really hold it, so to speak, but our faith holds us. We don't live with faith, but live through faith. Faith is that indefinable 'thing' that pleases God (Hebrews 11:6). It is how we truly see, how we truly hear, how we truly know, how we get back to Eden – now.

Just a side note: John the Baptist often gets a bad rap for doubting, but he did say, '... or should we expect another?' This guy did waver as to whether Jesus was the One, but he did not waver that the One was to come.

Believing in Jesus, and walking with Him, is a walk, not a talk. It is a humble walk. It can be lonely. It is gritty. It is uphill. It is pure, it is peace, it is joy.

## LIFE Activity:

Follow Jesus!

(Psalm 19:1-2; Amos 4:13; Isaiah 7:14; Isaiah 9:1-7; Isaiah 53; John 1:1-5; John 3:8; John 4:24; John 6:63; Mark 8:34-38; Luke 12:4-5, 8-9; Colossians 1:15-20; Hebrews 1:3; Hebrews 11:1, 6; II Corinthians 5:7)

## Videos

Let's face it, we're a screen generation! Here are a few short videos that may be encouraging, just speaking to some bible verses or themes. If you would like a whole lot more, you can subscribe to my YouTube channel, follow my Instagram, or whatever. The best way to get those links is to simply visit my website: www.1peter1three.weebly.com

**DEAR TEEN**

**TATTOOS AND THE BIBLE**

**PEER PRESSURE**

## Note from the Author

No devotional or other Christian reading should ever take the place of a disciplined reading of scripture. No other Christian 'stuff' will fortify your mind and soul – not bumper stickers, social media posts, verse stickers or scented stationery, positive thinking, youth groups, church meetings, worship songs, evangelical flavored coffee beverages... The 66 books that make up the bible are for here and now – not for when we are in heaven. Jesus quoted the bible a lot (Matthew 4:1-11; Luke 4:18, etc.), as did the apostles as can be seen throughout Acts. We are told it is the 'sword of the spirit' (that attacking piece of armor – Ephesians 6:17), and that it is sharper than a double-edge sword (Heb 4:12). Timothy is told that his knowledge of and instruction in the scriptures is what made him 'wise for salvation through faith in Jesus Christ' (II Timothy 3:15), and Paul goes on to say that scripture (referring at that time only to the Old Testament), is useful for *'teaching, rebuking, correcting and training in righteousness, so that the servant of God may be thoroughly equipped for every good work.'* (vs 16-17).

The church is weak and 'in error' today, as were the Sudducees then, because, as Jesus said we *'... do not know the Scriptures or the power of God'* (Matthew 22:29). Because of lack of *true* scripture knowledge – that laden with a love and pursuit of God, not just head knowledge and self-righteousness (John 5:39-40; Matthew 22:36-40; Deuteronomy 6:4-5; Leviticus 19:18) – the Sadducees overlooked the presence, person and power of Jesus in their midst, and actually approached him on silly, pseudo-theological matters. Does this sound like us today? What's the antidote? Get in the Word. Read it daily. Set aside time, designate a place, and put on the coffee! Make it a ritual. It will become the sweetest time of your day.

*'You keep in perfect peace, whose mind is staid on You.'* Isaiah 26:3

*For more information about Peter Walker, and for links to his YouTube channel, Instagram and Facebook page, visit:*
*www.1peter1three.weebly.com*

Made in the USA
Columbia, SC
28 August 2018